LIGHTNING
BOLT
BOOKS™

Where Do We Keep MONEY?

Jennifer S. Larson

How Banks Work

Lerner Publications Company

Minneapolis

For Cheyenne
and Riley

Lerner Publications Company
A division of Lerner Publishing Group, Inc.
241 First Avenue North
Minneapolis, MN 55401 U.S.A.

Website address: www.lernerbooks.com

Library of Congress Cataloging-in-Publication Data

Larson, Jennifer S., 1967–
    Where do we keep money? : how banks work / by Jennifer S. Larson.
        p.   cm. — (Lightning bolt books™—Exploring economics)
    Includes index.
    ISBN 978-0-7613-3911-3 (lib. bdg. : alk. paper)
    1. Banks and banking—Juvenile literature. I. Title.
HG1609.L37 2010
332.1—dc22   2009027467

Manufactured in the United States of America
1 — BP — 12/15/09

Contents

What is a Bank?

Have you
ever been
inside a
bank?

RIGGS NATIONAL BANK

FARM

This big bank is in
Washington, D.C.

A bank is a business that keeps our money for us.

This is the inside of a bank.

What's inside a bank? Well, there's money! The bank puts money in vaults to keep it safe. A vault is a special room with a big metal door.

Security guards work
at banks. They watch
over the vaults. They
also keep the people at
the bank safe.

Bank Accounts

Many other people work at banks. A bank worker can help you set up a bank account.

When you set up a bank account, you arrange to keep your money in a bank. Do you have a bank account?

A checking account is one kind of bank account. When someone opens a checking account, the bank gives that person checks. A check is a piece of paper that the person can use to buy things.

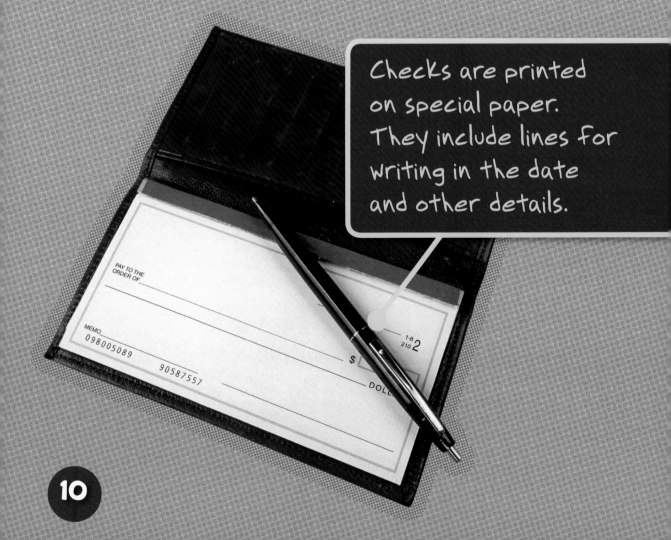

Checks are printed on special paper. They include lines for writing in the date and other details.

PAY TO THE
ORDER OF

MEMO
098005089

90587557

$

1-8
210 2

DOLL

When the person uses a check, the bank takes money from the person's account. The money is used to pay for things the person wants to buy.

This man is writing a check to pay for items at a store.

A savings account is another kind of bank account. Savings accounts are used for saving money.

Many people use booklets to keep track of the money in their savings accounts.

When you put money in a savings account, you usually get more money! That's because most banks pay interest. Interest is money a bank gives you for keeping your savings at the bank.

The more money you put in a savings account, the more money you earn.

Making Transactions

Tellers work behind the counter at banks. They can help you make a transaction. A transaction is a change to your bank account.

Deposits and withdrawals are two types of transactions. Putting money into your account is called a deposit. Taking money out is called a withdrawal.

Tellers count your money during a transaction. Then they record the transaction on a computer.

The teller will give you a receipt after your transaction. The receipt tells you how much money you put in or took out of your account.

Banks also send statements. A bank statement is a letter that tells you how much money is in your account.

CHECKS PAID		SUBTRACTIONS		INTEREST PD	BALANCE
O.	AMOUNT	NO.	AMOUNT		
3	784.00	46	2,731.75	0.10	1,120.97

COUNT ACTIVITY

DEPOSITS, INTEREST & OTHER ADDITIONS	CHECKS & OTHER SUBTRACTIONS	DAILY BALANCE
	503.00	$940.07
783.43	252.00	437.07
		185.07
	102.00	
	58.16	
		866.50
	0.50	
	40.43	

This line shows how much money is in this account.

Many banks put statements on their websites. People can read their statements on their home computers.

Many people use ATMs. ATM stands for automated teller machine.

An ATM can do some of the same things a bank teller can do. People use ATMs to make withdrawals or deposits. You have to have a bank account to use an ATM.

You need a secret code number to use an ATM. The number is called a PIN. PIN stands for personal identification number.

Loans

Does the money in your bank account just sit at the bank? No! The bank uses it. But don't worry. You can get your money back when you need it.

This girl has taken some money out of her account.

Banks use our money to help people in the community. A family might want to buy something big, such as a house. They will borrow money from the bank.

This family just bought a house. They borrowed the money from the bank.

The money borrowed from a bank is called a loan.

This woman is a loan officer. She helps people figure out how much to borrow.

People must repay banks for loans. Most people repay a little money every month. It might take years to repay a big loan.

Credit Cards

Did you know that using a credit card is like getting a loan? A credit card is a plastic card that people use to buy things.

Credit card bills can be paid online. Or they can be paid by sending a check to the bank.

Many people get credit cards from banks. The bank pays for things that people buy with credit cards. Then the people must repay the bank.

Activities
Interest

Pretend you have a bank account that earns interest. You have $100 in your account.

The first year, you earn $3 in interest. The second year, you earn $3.50. How much interest did you make in two years? How much is in your account?

Interest earned

First year $3.00
Second year + $3.50
            = total interest

total interest
+ $100.00
= amount in your account

(Answers appear in the bottom right-hand corner.)

Your Account

Pretend you have a savings account at a bank. You started with $50.

You withdrew $10 to buy your sister a birthday present.

Then you made a deposit to your account. You added $12 that you made at a lemonade stand.

How much money do you have now?

(Answer appears in the bottom left-hand corner.)

$50.00
- $10.00
+ $12.00
──────────
=amount in your account

Glossary

ATM: an automated teller machine. An ATM can do some of the same things a bank teller can do.

bank: a business that keeps our money for us

bank account: an arrangement to keep money in a bank

bank statement: a letter that tells you how much money is in your account

check: a piece of paper that a person can use to buy things

credit card: a plastic card that people use to buy things. Using a credit card is like getting a loan.

deposit: putting money into a bank account

interest: money a bank gives you for keeping your savings at the bank

loan: money borrowed from a bank

teller: a person who works behind the counter at a bank

transaction: a change to your bank account

vault: a special room with a big metal door. Banks put money in vaults to keep it safe.

withdrawal: taking money out of a bank account

Further Reading

The Banking Kids Page
http://www.bankingkids.com/pages/elem.html

It's My Life: Money
http://pbskids.org/itsmylife/money/index.html

Johnston, Marianne. *Let's Visit the Bank.* New York: PowerKids Press, 2000.

Larson, Jennifer S. *What Can You Do with Money?: Earning, Spending, and Saving.* Minneapolis: Lerner Publications Company, 2010.

Zamosky, Lisa. *Bank Tellers: Then and Now.* Huntington Beach, CA: Teacher Created Materials, 2008.

Index

Photo Acknowledgments

The images in this book are used with the permission of: © Anderson Ross/Blend Images/Getty Images, p. 2; © Chuck Pefley/Alamy, p. 4; © Merten/StockphotoPro.com, p. 5; © Mira/Alamy, p. 6; Reflexstock, p. 7; Sigrid Olsson/PhotoAlto agency RF/Getty images, p. 8; © INSADCO Photography/Alamy, p. 9; © Creatas/Photolibrary, p. 10; © Dan Dalton/Photolibrary, p. 11; © Todd Strand/Independent Picture Service, pp. 12, 22; iStockphoto.com/© Lisa Thornberg, p. 13; © Jason Dewey/Taxi/Getty Images, p. 14; © Comstock Images/Getty Images, p. 15; © Ryan McVay/Photodisc/Getty Images, p. 16; © David R. Frazier Photolibrary, Inc. /StockphotoPro.com, p. 17; © Seankate/Dreamstime.com, p. 18; © Big Cheese /Photolibrary, p. 19; © Andrew Rubtsov/Alamy, p. 20; © Hans Eder/StockphotoPro.com, p. 21; Reflexstock/Kablonk RF, p. 23; © iStockphoto.com/Jeffery Smith, p. 24; Reflexstock/Corbis RF, p. 25; Reflexstock/© PhotoAlto/Eric Audras, p. 26; © Fancy/Photolibrary, p. 27; © iStockphoto.com/gaffera, p. 29 (top); © iStockphoto.com/jkbowers, p. 29 (bottom); Comstock Images/Getty Images, p. 31.

Front cover: © Todd Strand/Independent Picture Service.